To Nadine D'
You in Perfe

PLEZE RAYBON

SANCTIFY
-John
THEM BY

YOUR WORD
17:17-
IS TRUTH

The Extended Version

"TRUTHFUL LIPS ENDURE FOREVER BUT A
LYING TONGUE LASTS ONLY A MOMENT."

-PROVERBS 12:19

CONTENTS

ACKNOWLEDGMENT 1

INTRODUCTION 2

THE GAP THEORY 3

   LET'S GO A LITTLE DEEPER:
     ADAM AND EVE. 6

   LET'S GO A LITTLE DEEPER:
     HINDSIGHT IS 20/20! 11

   LET'S GO A LITTLE DEEPER:
     BROKEN. 17

   LET'S GO A LITTLE DEEPER:
     A RAMPART OF LOVE 21

LET'S GO A LITTLE DEEPER:
A RAMPART OF HATE 23

LET'S GO A LITTLE DEEPER:
EXPOSING THE ILL'S OF
THE SOUL. 26

LET'S GO A LITTLE DEEPER:
FOREORDAINED 28

LET'S GO A LITTLE DEEPER:
REALLY!!? 30

LET'S GO A LITTLE DEEPER:
THE OBJECTIVE OF
GOD AND SATAN 32

LET'S GO A LITTLE DEEPER:
THE ABSTRACT METHOD
OF THE ENEMY. 35

LET'S GO A LITTLE DEEPER:
WHY SUBMIT? 40

LET'S GO A LITTLE DEEPER:
WHY RESIST? 41

LET GO A LITTLE DEEPER:
INORDINATE AFFECTION. 43

LET'S GO A LITTLE DEEPER:
PROVERBS 6:16 THESE SIX
THINGS GOD HATES AND
SEVEN IS AN ABOMINATION. . . . 46

LET'S GO A LITTLE DEEPER:
A LYING TONGUE, AND
HANDS THAT SHED
INNOCENT BLOOD 48

LET'S GO A LITTLE DEEPER:
WHAT IS SATAN REALLY
AFTER? Faith & Love! 53

LET'S GO A LITTLE DEEPER:
THE MISCONCEPTION OF
FAITH. 59

LET'S GO A LITTLE DEEPER:
UNSHAKABLE FAITH OF
NOAH AND ABRAHAM. 65

IN CLOSING:
THE JUDGEMENT. 71

iv

ACKNOWLEDGMENT

I thank God for the prayers of my two brothers: Rev. Fred McGirt and John Raybon. My two sisters: Joyce and Helen Raybon. My two beautiful children: Melea and Jesse Raybon, I love, love, love you both!

INTRODUCTION

Acts 17:11

These Bereans were more noble than those in Thessalonica, in that they received the word of God with all readiness of mind, searching and examining the scriptures daily, to see if these things were so.

It would be beneficial, if we the people of God had that same attitude. There are a lot of different things being said, and many different teachings.

I understand that we have different revelations, and insights, but some of these insights, and revelations can be misleading. There are many insights, and revelations: but only one absolute truth! There are many questionable opinions: but only one absolute fact! So I have learned to study to show myself approved unto God, because therein lies the absolute truth.

According to the truth, I can refute some of these teachings that are misleading.

THE GAP THEORY

There are some who teaches that there was a thousand year gap in Genesis chapter 1 between verses 1 & 2. They claim, this is the results of Satan being cast out of heaven; causing chaos, confusion, and disorder. These teachers agree that God created the Heavens, and the Earth, but it was destroyed when Satan was cast out of heaven. Which is not true!

One minister said, God doesn't create anything void, and how can he create darkness, if there's no darkness in him? They didn't stop there, they use one more scripture to try and prove a point. Genesis 1:28: "And God blessed them, and said unto them be fruitful, and multiply, and replenish the earth and subdue it." I guess they were confused by the word replenish, because they are saying it means to refill.

Let's see what the truth has to say about all of that! God the Father created the Heavens, and the Earth, and they are right on this one issue, He doesn't make anything void.

Is it so hard to believe it was dark because God hadn't spoken the sun, moon, and stars into existence, and it was void or empty because God hadn't put anything on it yet? The term replenish: If you look at the Hebrew definition, you will find the word (maw-law) it means to fill or be full of. Maybe that is too simple for some, and maybe they are basing it on 2nd Peter 3:8 which says: "Be not ignorant of this one thing, that one day is with the Lord as a thousand years, and a thousand years as one day." Maybe they are basing it on, Psalm 90:4 It says, "For a thousand years in thy sight are but as yesterday when it is past, and as a watch in the night."

You must understand those scriptures are talking about God, and time is not a factor to Him. The truth is, time is a factor to us, and if you notice, when He was creating the world He made it clear, that it was six literal days by stating, "The evening, and the morning was the first day". Exodus 20:11 says: "For in six days the Lord made the heaven and earth, the sea, and all that in them is, and rested on the seventh day"... If you look carefully at verses 1 & 2 of Genesis chapter 1, you will see the trinity at work.

- God the Father created the heavens and the earth. How did he do it? With the word! Who is the word? Jesus!
- Listen to the truth of scripture. Ephesians 3:9: and to make all men see what is the fellowship of the mystery, which was from the beginning of the world has been hid in God, who <u>created</u> all things by <u>Jesus</u> <u>Christ</u>.
- Colossians 1:16: For by Him (Jesus) were all things created, that are in heaven, and that are in earth, visible and invisible, whether they be thrones, or dominions, or principalities, or powers: all things were created by Him, and for him.

Before we go any farther: I want to show you one key word, that blows that teaching away, That key word is 'And', We know that the word 'And' is a continuation of a phrase. It's used three

- THE TRUTH: THE EXTENDED VERSION -

times in that verse, the last one being key: <u>And the Spirit of God moved</u> upon the face of the waters. The Hebrew word moved is (raw-khaf), it means to brood. What is the purpose of brooding? A chicken broods over her eggs for what purpose? To bring forth life! What is the role of the Holy Spirit? To Quicken or give life.

The minister that said, how can God create darkness if there's no darkness in Him, has not read the truth of Isaiah 45:7. It says: "I form the light, and create darkness: I make peace, and create evil: I the Lord, do all these things."

Please read Genesis chapter 2 starting with verse 4-8, God gave us a full history of the heavens, and the earth when they were created. The Father never said anything about a gap! If God didn't reveal it, why are some trying to teach it as truth?

Deuteronomy 29:29 says: "The secret things belong unto the Lord our God: but those things which are revealed belong to us, and to our children forever, that we may do all the words of this law." Everything God wants us to know is in His word.

This is a violation of scripture! They are adding to the word of God. There are many scriptures that deals with this issue, but I like the simplicity of Proverbs 30:5&6, it says: "Every word Of God is pure: He is a shield unto them that put their trust in him. V6 Add thou not unto his words, lest He reprove you, and you be found a liar."

LET'S GO A LITTLE DEEPER: ADAM AND EVE

I have heard so many different views, on what happened in the case of Adam and Eve. I could never accept what they were teaching. They make it sound as if Adam was standing right next to her (Eve), listening to the whole conversation, and didn't say anything. But when you look closely, and pay attention to what is said, the truth is right there, you don't have to assume anything.

So let's see what happened: I could dive right into this, but I would like to set the stage.

Genesis 1:26: God said let <u>US: FATHER, SON, and SPIRIT,</u> (<u>tripart God</u>); make man in our image, <u>Spirit</u>, <u>Soul</u> and <u>Body</u>, (<u>a tripart Being</u>). Then He equipped us saying: after our likeness. Giving us the ability to create, to love, to show mercy, and kindness, to have compassion. Notice He didn't say let us have dominion, but let them have dominion over the fish, birds, cattle, over all the earth, and over every creeping thing that creeps upon the earth.

When you correlate that with Psalms 115:16 you will get a better understanding. It says, "The heavens belongs to the Lord, but

- THE TRUTH: THE EXTENDED VERSION -

He has given the earth to the sons of Adam. The word dominion means: to rule! God gave the earth to man to rule, and manage it. Now think about this: God has given man the earth, so what is the purpose of the garden?

(...A time for testing)

It is important to understand that Genesis is the book of beginnings; in it, you will see the first of everything. Genesis 2:8: "The Lord God planted a garden eastward in Eden; and there He put the man whom he had formed. *V9* Out of the ground the Lord God made every tree that's pleasant to the eye, and good for food; the tree of life in the midst of the garden, and the tree of the knowledge of good and evil. *V16* The Lord God commanded the man, saying, Of every tree of the garden you may freely eat: *V17* But of the tree of the knowledge of good and evil, you shall not eat of it: for in the day that you eat of it you shall surely die."

Let's go past him naming all the animals, God put before him to name, because after naming them; he didn't have a help meet for himself.

God put the man into a deep sleep, and took from his side a rib, and made for him a suitable help meet. Here are three things I want you to see!

1. It is not recorded in scripture, that Adam told Eve about the command God gave to him, telling him, not to eat from the tree of the knowledge of good and evil.

2. When you read her response to the serpent: it is obvious he did tell her.

- PLEZE RAYBON -

3.   You will see the woman, usurping authority over the man.

According to Genesis 3:1: she was approached by the most cunning, and craftiest, creature God had made. He, (the serpent) goes to the women, questioning her about the command God gave to her husband; but he changed two words just to get her engaged.

The original command was: you <u>may</u> freely eat from <u>every</u> tree of the garden, but not from the tree of the knowledge of good and evil. The serpent says to her, "Can it really be that God has said, You <u>shall not</u> eat from <u>every</u> tree of the garden? Her response was like any normal Human Being, when words are changed in a question; she tries to correct him, which proves she was told, saying "We may eat of the fruit from the trees of the garden, but not from the tree that's in the midst of the garden, God said you shall not eat of it, or touch it lest you die.

Satan lured her in just to tell her the truth. I know some of you are probably saying: Satan is the father of lies, he can not tell the truth, and I agree with you! But when you correlate, 1st Corinthians 15:46 with that; you will get a better understanding. It says, "That is not first which is <u>spiritual</u> but that which is <u>NATURAL</u> and after that, that which is <u>spiritual</u>." He (Satan) told her the truth in the natural: saying to her "you will not die: For God knows that in the day you eat of it, your eyes will be opened, and you will be like God, knowing good and evil."

I will repeat: her response to Satan's question proves that Adam had told her not to eat from that tree. The words came out of her mouth. Here is where you will see the woman <u>USURPING AUTHORITY</u> over the man. I'm going to give you the definition

- THE TRUTH: THE EXTENDED VERSION -

first: To seize and hold, as the power, position, or rights of another, But focus on the word (seize), it means, to take away or gain control or possession of. She did what she was told not to do!

She saw that the tree was good for food, and that it was pleasant to the eyes, and to make one wise. She took of it's fruit and ate; and she gave some also to her husband with her, and he ate. Then their eyes were opened, and they knew they were naked. Now that's how I've heard it explained: they leave you with the impression that he (Adam) was standing right next to her, hearing the whole conversation, and didn't say anything. I just could not accept that!

Then reading it again, from the Amplified bible: I saw something that made sense. Again, I have read some of the commentaries, and they make a good point, and they are very thorough, but they are leaving out one key element that unlocks the truth. In this case: it is the (semicolon). We know that a comma is a pause, but still related to the same scenario. But a semicolon is greater than a pause, it's more like a brake, but still related to the same scenario or plot. So yes! he was in the garden with her: but the semicolon, indicates she had time to walk a distance, probably still chewing on the fruit as she was approaching him.

Imagine now, what Adam was thinking, being told by God, for in the day that you eat from that tree, you shall surely die, and here comes Mrs. Eve, walking toward him chewing on the fruit, and she don't look faintish, and based on what God said in Genesis 3:17: she persuaded him to partake of the fruit. I want you to take note again, to the definition, (to seize): "to take away or gain control." Then listen to God's response, saying, "because you listen to your <u>wife</u> and <u>ate</u> of the tree of which <u>I commanded</u> you not to eat of, <u>cursed</u> be the ground because of you."

How do I know that Satan told her the truth (In the natural)? The answer is in verse 22, "And the Lord God said, Behold or look, the man has become like one of us, knowing good and evil." Here is an obvious point: our Father did not want us to know evil, only good. Why? Because our Daddy knows that in the natural, evil prevails, just as it has done. Matthew 7:13: "Enter in at the strait gate: for wide is the gate, and broad is the way, that leads to destruction," that evil way; and many have found it.

He, (God) continues saying, "Lest he put forth his hand, and take also of the tree of life, and eat, and live forever in that sinful state." God removed the man from the garden, and placed Cherubims, and a flaming sword which turned every way to guard the tree of life.

LET'S GO A LITTLE DEEPER: HINDSIGHT IS 20/20!

I wanted to understand why we have so many divorces, so many abured Women, and so many abured Men. Let me clarify: I am not talking to the unbeliever, because according to Ephesians 2:1: they are still dead in trespasses and sins.

I'm talking to people that go to church, expressing their love to the Father, with their hands lifted up, saying I Love you Lord. Then leave the church and fight on the way home. Even Pastors, the over seers of the local Church, 'The worse': Some of them are reprobabed.

When a Pastor can stand, and preach the word of God; then have sex with his secretary; – then go home and be with his wife. Then come back, and stand before the people of God, and Preach the word, that is a reprobated mind to the highest degree!!

Hopefully this insight will bring some clarity to why we have so many divorces; and hopefully prevent you, the reader from getting one.

I have played for a lot of weddings, and I see the look of Happiness, and Joy on their faces, and they want that marriage to succeed, especially the woman. Then you see one of them a year or two later, and they are divorced.

I have been divorced twice, and, some of you might be saying: two failed marriages Brother, how can you tell me anything? I'm hoping you will see what I saw; which is God's view on the subject. The B part of Proverbs 4:7 says: "in all thy getting get an understanding." When you understand the why and the reasons of a matter, it gives you more fighting power, not against one another: but against the enemy that comes to kill, steal, and destroy. I'm mainly talking to believers!

Ladies, I will be addressing you first because God does, and it's going to sound like I am against you; but you have to see God's view.

Ladies: most of, and possibly all of you, don't understand why you have an issue with, even the sound of control or restrictions. I'm going to call this 'The women Issue' and the women issue started with the command, God gave to her husband Adam in Genesis 2:16. We covered all of that in the previous topic.

Genesis 3:1 says: "the serpent was more subtle or crafty than any living creature God had made." I'm going to rephrase this statement; so you can see how crafty he is. He (Satan) goes to the woman questioning her about the command God gave to her husband, but he changed two words; causing her to ignore what she was told.

The truth is: she usurped authority over her husband. Let me give you the definition of the word usurped: Take the place of

- THE TRUTH: THE EXTENDED VERSION -

someone in a position of power illegally; supplant. To seize and hold (office, place, functions, powers etc.) Take possession by force or without right. Please understand this: what you see in a person, it is what they developed into based on the judgment God placed on them in Genesis 3:16. After He told the woman how she was going to suffer through childbearing, He said, "Yet your desire and craving will be for your Husband."

That sounds like a good thing, but when you look at the Hebrew word [tesh-oo-kaw]; you will see that it's not. That word desire means, 'a stretching out after; a longing.' But it derived from the word [shook], which means to run after or over i.e. overflow, in other words, to seize. It is that same spirit, that has mutated into trickery, and manipulation. Then it says, "but he will rule over you" (the woman). That word 'rule' has the connotation of male-centered, or Androcentric, male dominance. That spirit; mutated into exploitation, in many forms: The act of treating someone unfairly for your gain, or benefit.

Let's look at some scriptures and see what the woman developed into. Proverbs 21:9, it says: "it is better to dwell in the corner of a housetop [on a flat oriental roof], than in a house shared with a nagging, quarrelsome, and faultfinding woman." The same chapter, verse 19 "It is better to dwell in a desert land, than with a contentious woman with vexation." (The act of being frustrated).

(Amp Bible) – The Preacher says in Ecclesiastes 7:25: "I turned about [penitent] and my heart was set to know and to search out and to seek [true] wisdom and the reason of things, and to know that wickedness is folly, and that foolishness is madness, and what had led me into such wickedness and madness. *V26* I found that [of all sinful follies none has been so ruinous in seducing one away from God as the idolatrous women] more bitter than death is the woman whose heart is snares, and nets, and whose hands are bands. He that please God shall escape from her, but the sinner shall be taken by her." I will repeat, – that is not why she was 'MADE'; that is what she developed into; through many forms of trauma, heart break, no good father figure in the home, a life without God.

Brothers, you might have had a father, that was a womanizer, abusive, physically and verbally. You as a child didn't know why Mom and Dad was fighting, and you hated seeing your dad beat your Mom; but when you became of age, with no understanding, you probably said, now I see why my dad was beating her. But that is not why he was FORMED.

Isaiah 43:7, Shows us the true purpose we were created for: "Even everyone who is called by my name. Whom I have created for MY GLORY, whom I have FORMED, whom I have MADE." God FORMED man from the dust of the ground; and He MADE the woman from the rib of the man. Then sin and death entered into the world, and according to Ecclesiastes 7:29, it says: "behold, this is the only reason for it that I have found: God made man upright, but they the man, and the woman, have sought out many devices for evil." Doing whatever felt right to them!

Now let's go to the redemptive side of all this with the TRUTH. Our Father God knows what we've been through, so He deals with the origin of our issues.

Ephesians 5:21: "Submitting yourselves one to another in the fear of the Lord." That is the key! Because when you do that, there will be no arguing, no slammed doors, no physical or verbal abuse. 1st Timothy 2:14, says: "...It was not Adam who was deceived, but the woman", so God deals with the woman first

- THE TRUTH: THE EXTENDED VERSION -

saying in verse 22: "Wives, submit yourselves unto your own husbands, as a service the Lord." WHY?

V23 "Because the husband is the head of the wife, even as Christ is the head of the church: and he is the saviour of the body. *V24* "Therefore as the church is subject unto Christ, so let the wives be to their own husbands in <u>EVERYTHING</u>."

Now, if you understand those scriptures; and choose not to obey them: then you are usurping authority over the man; and you are suppressing his manhood or authority, and preventing his development, in the role of a husband.

Christ is the head of man, and if he's submitted to Christ: he will become the man you never thought possible.

God tell us how to love one another, *V25* God tells the man how to love his wife; "which is to love her the way Christ loved the Church and died for it." Verse 28 says: "to love her the way you love yourself, he who loves his wife loves himself." *V29* "No man ever hated his own flesh, but nourishes, and carefully protects, and cherishes it, as Christ does the Church."

Notice how verse 31 takes us back to Genesis 2:24, before sin and death entered into the world, He's showing us His original plan: The two shall become one flesh.

'BROTHERS' If you don't know the purpose of something; you will abuse it. So please give this your undivided attention! God made her to be a suitable help meet. The Hebrew word for <u>meet</u> is 'Ezer' which means: to aid; to help, but it derived from the word 'Azer', which means: to surround, i.e. protect or aid. My point is brothers: When we were single, we developed many blind spots that only we had to deal with. But now you are married, and you might need help in areas you are not aware of, and shes there to surround you with love and respect, to help, to aid and protect you.

I'm sure you can do it, but I don't think you would feel completely safe doing it, – driving a car without rear-view or side-view mirrors. Even with side-view mirrors, a car can be in that blind spot, and you won't see it. That is the role of the help meet, she see things you don't see.

This is where you take heed to verse 21, submitting yourselves one to another in the fear of the Lord. Then you won't get offended, when she points out some things you don't see, and because you are submitting to each other in the fear of the Lord: There should never be yelling or a raised voice. For one, it is disrespectful, and two, you are not accomplishing anything, because you are ignoring the art of communicating; one talks while the other listens. I mean truly listen; not sitting there waiting for your turn to say something.

Proverbs 13:10 shows us what causes contention or arguing, it says, ... "By pride and insolence comes only contention, but with the well-advised is skillful and godly wisdom." I know you have heard Ephesians 5:21-33, but you need to know how to get the results, in this next topic we will deal with that!

LET'S GO A LITTLE DEEPER: BROKEN

Matthew 21:44: "whosoever shall fall on this stone will be broken: but on whomsoever it shall fall, it will grind him to powder."

I cry a lot, I even cry when I see touching commercials. My point is: tears has nothing to do with brokenness, but everything to do with righteousness, obedience and trust. That is the basis of that chapter; but I want to give you my insight on what true brokenness is!

The word Broken means: to crush, to dash together, i.e. shatter: – break. Then when you follow the trail of definitions; you will see, it denotes Union with, and it has other applications including, completeness.

Psalms 32:9 says: "Be not like the horse or the mule, which lack understanding, which must have their mouths held firm with bit, and bridle or else they will not come with you." But I want to use the horse to illustrate my point, and hopefully; bring some clarity to what it means to be broken.

An individual purchases a wild horse: one that's never been ridden before. Before the horse can be of any benefit to the owner; the horse must be broken.

This is a violent undertaking; but when the horse is broken, the first thing that takes place is obedience. You can now order the horse to go left or right, fast or slow, and come to a complete stop, just by using the reins; and over a period of time trust is established.

This is when union and completeness is recognized: meaning, you can now put blinder on the horse, because he is now being guided by your eyes, and you turn him where you want to go, that is genuine trust!

We came into the Kingdom of God, wild and untamed: with no spiritual understanding. Accepting him was the easy part. But trusting him; it's going to take some crushing, dashing together, shatter, to eradicate your carnal and natural way of thinking; to truly trusting in Him, leaning not to your own understanding.

But like that wild horse, you will be trying your best, to resist the spiritual life you've been born into; But when understanding comes, and there is no resistance, and you agree with, and welcome the words of the Lord in Psalms 32:8, when He says: "I [the Lord] will instruct you and teach you in the way you should go; I will counsel you or guide you with My eye upon you."

Did you get that? You know how much money people spend on marriage counseling. But God said, I will counsel you with My eyes on you. This is for those that want to do it His way.

- THE TRUTH: THE EXTENDED VERSION -

Understand this: He has the panoramic view, and we know He leads and guides us into all truths. That's when you are in union with Him, following His lead or instructions.

Understand this also: this is a willful act, not a stumble. There should come a time when you realize that your way is not working; Then you fall on that stone, and be broken; and let the truth of God's word put you back together. But if that stone falls on you; it will grind you to powder. This is someone who chooses to trust in himself. Usurping authority over the Lord ship of Christ, that is considered wicked, and he or she, will experience Psalms 32:10 it says: "many are the sorrows of the wicked, but he who trust in the Lord shall be compassed about with mercy and with loving-kindness."

When you do it Gods way; you will get Gods results. Ecclesiastes 7:8 says: "Better is the end of a thing than the beginning of it, and the patient in spirit is better than the proud in spirit."

The patient in spirit, are the ones that obey His word, and they know that it is an uphill journey. When they hit a rough spot, they submit themselves one to another in the fear of the Lord, then God the father strengthens them, and they continue to move forward, (they are not trying it, they are doing it)! When you do it Gods way, the results are guaranteed to be good.

But the proud in spirit, they try it; and when they hit a rough spot, they go back to doing it their way, and the results are guaranteed to be sorrowful.

If you want the good: do it His way, If you don't do it His way; (automatic defeat). God wants His children to walk in victory in every area, especially the marriage union. Ephesians 5:32 says:

- PLEZE RAYBON -

"This mystery is very great, but I speak concerning [the relation of Christ and the Church]."

That's how important this union is in the sight of our Heavenly Father. He compares it to Christ and the Church. Why? To bring forth a Godly seed.

LET'S GO A LITTLE DEEPER: A RAMPART OF LOVE

Let's start with the definition of Rampart: It means, an embankment, built for defense, or anything that serves as a defense, protection, or an elevation. Now let's go to the word of God and since we're focusing on the Rampart of Love; let's look at Gods position, method, and phraseology, and His love for the simple. We can safely say that wisdom typifies Jesus!

Scripture says in 1st Corinthians 1:30: "Jesus is made unto us Wisdom, Sanctification, and Redemption."

Let's begin in the book of (KJV) Proverbs 9:1-6 which states: "Wisdom has built her house, She has hewn out her seven pillars: $V2$ She has killed her beasts; she has mingled her wine; she has also furnished her table. $V3$ She has sent forth her maidens: She cries upon the highest places of the city. $V4$ Whoso is simple, let him turn in hither; as for him that want understanding, she says to him, come, eat of my bread, and drink of the wine which I have mingled. Forsake the foolish and live; and go in the way of understanding." Look at verse 3 again, it says, "she cries upon the highest places, or mound, or an elevation of the city – to give wise and sound instructions to the simple. Wisdom is telling us to eat of the bread, and drink of the wine, which she has mingled.

This typify Jesus, because He is the bread of life. It also typify the Holy Spirit: because He is the only one who can satisfy our thirst for righteousness. Most importantly of all, it tells the simple, how to acquire wisdom, and understanding. Listen to how the Amplified Bible reads in Proverbs 9:10: "The reverent and worshipful fear of the Lord is the beginning, the chief, and choice part of wisdom, and the knowledge of the Holy one is insight and understanding."

The fear of the Lord, is the beginning of wisdom, but it is the knowledge of God, that gives you insight, and understanding. 2nd Peter 1:13: "According as his divine power hath given unto us all things that pertain unto life and godliness, through the knowledge of Him that called us to glory and virtue." (Please continue to read verses 4-11) it will benefit you!

Take note to the Places from where wisdom speaks: the highest places of the city. Her method: Her words, and phraseology: the way it's said, and whom she's addressing, the simple.

The purpose of wisdom; is to build a wall of protection around the simple, with the truth; to elevate them to a higher place, and God has given us His Spirit to take us to that higher place. Ephesians 2:6 says it like this: "God has raised us up together, and made us sit together in heavenly places in Christ Jesus." To deliver the simple from the corruption that is in the world through lust; and to give them the abundant life and an expected or hopeful end.

LET'S GO A LITTLE DEEPER: A RAMPART OF HATE

In contrast to wisdom, the foolish woman typify the world, or the spirit of wickedness. According to Proverbs 9:13-17: "She is clamorous or loud: She is simple, and knows nothing. *V14* she sits at the door of her house on a seat in the high places of the city, *V15* to call passengers who go right on their ways: *V16* Whoso is simple, let him turn in hither: (Him that is wavering and easily led astray), and as for him that want understanding, she says to him, *V17* stolen waters are sweet and bread eaten in secret is pleasant." She's saying that forbidden pleasures, or that which is done in secret is pleasant. She gives the simple nothing but a harder way to go! But that's the world, it's big, it's loud, and it offers many opportunities; that leads to destruction, and false hope.

Even the Psalmist A'saph talks about how his feet almost slipped: looking at the prosperity of the wicked. Psalms 73:2, But in verse 17 he said, "until I went into the sanctuary of God; then I understood their end." (Please read that whole Psalms)!

- PLEZE RAYBON -

You must understand, everything Satan does: it is to distract you from receiving the truth. Even showering you with false riches.

Proverbs 8:18: "God our Father gives them that love Him 'durable riches' His love and promise of eternal life."

It is important to note: that she the (wicked women) is talking to the simple, and as they are unaware of Satan's plans, they unknowingly go into destruction.

To make matters even worse, when they look to the Church, they hear of Pastors having sex with their secretaries. Pastors coming out of the closet, having sex with other men. Children being sexually abused, a higher divorce rate in the Church, than that of the world! The simple don't know, that wide is the gate; and broad is the way that leads to destruction. So they continue down broad way where everyone seems to be having a good time. Proverbs 9:18 says: "they don't know that the dead are there; and her guests are in the depths of hell."

Take a look at verse 3 again: and you will see that God placed wisdom in the highest places of the city. Wisdom cries to the simple, forsake the foolish in live and go in the way of understanding. Children of God, the Church is suppose to be a bright light; to draw them that go on their ways. But her light has become so dim, the simple don't even notice it.

The foolish woman, which typifies the world, has the attention of the simple. Not because she has a bright light, or even the goods: but because she is loud. She doesn't need to be in the highest places to get their attention. She knows that she can keep them entertained by magnifying all the bad things that's happening in the Church, and keep them distracted with noise.

- THE TRUTH: THE EXTENDED VERSION -

Look at the kid today: their music is so loud it will have your car vibrating ten feet away. It's the noise that keeps them distracted and the dimming light of the Church: keeps them confused. The simple, in their confusion will try to fill that void with everything accept the Truth, and Jesus is the Way, the <u>Truth</u> and the life, and he is the only one who can feel that void. This is why it is so important to have a personal and vibrant relationship with God the Holy Spirit through our Lord Jesus Christ; to help them see the Truth! Because Satan's sole purpose is to build an embankment of misery, and despair, even as a believer.

I do believe Christians need to hear this again and again. Why? Because I have talked to many Christians, and they don't seem to understand or have a clue to what Satan is after, and we will deal with that later.

LET'S GO A LITTLE DEEPER: EXPOSING THE ILL'S OF THE SOUL.

The <u>Truth</u> is the only thing that exposes all the ills of the soul.

Paul said in Romans 7:7-8: "I had not known sin, but by the law: I had not known lust, until the law said thou shall not covet." It was verse 8 that revealed the power of sin: "But sin taking opportunity by the Commandments, wrought in me all manner of concupiscence." 'Concupiscence': a interesting word, this word stresses the lust, Cravings, Longings, or Desires for what is usually forbidden. It is an irrational longing for pleasure, unbridled lust. Now that opens up a whole spectrum of things that I will not expound on. But the tenth commandment exposes all of what only God can see.

Without the commandments sin was dead, Romans 5:13: "…Until the Law sin was in the world, but sin is not Imputed when there's no Law." The purpose of the Law or commandments: were to show man-kind his boundaries; because his ways were offensive to God! The commandments fulfilled its purposes, which was to show man-kind the power of sin.

- THE TRUTH: THE EXTENDED VERSION -

I will repeat Romans 7:8: (AMP) "But sin, finding opportunity in the commandment [to express itself], got a hold on me and aroused and stimulated all kinds of forbidden desires (lust, covetousness)." Please study Romans, Chapter 7, it will give you a better understanding.

Man judges the outward appearance: we look at people, and we think, or say, they are this or that. But God judges the heart; and this is what God said, in Jeremiah 17:9-10: "The heart is deceitful above all things. (We can fool the people), and desperately wicked: (it can devise all kind of wicked plans or Schemes), who can know the heart? *V10* I the Lord search the heart, and try the reins, even to give to every man according to his ways, and according to the fruit of his doing."

But our God is full of compassion: He said in Ezekiel 36:26-27: "A new heart also will I give you, and a new spirit will I put within you: and I will take away the stony heart out of your flesh, and give you a heart of flesh. *V27* ...and I will put my Spirit within you, and cause you to walk in my statues, and you shall keep my judgments, and do them." The only thing that will take us to that place, is obedience to His word, which is the absolute Truth.

We play a big rolled in this process by studying to show ourselves approved unto God. His word will give us the victory over these three forces: 1) The lust of the flesh: that is a craving for sensual gratification. 2) The lust of the eyes: Greedy longings of the mind. 3) The pride of life: The assurance in one's own resources or in the stability of earthly things. That is the scope of his arsenal, but it is very vast, especially to the carnal minds.

LET'S GO A LITTLE DEEPER: FOREORDAINED

Scripture has pointed out, that Jesus was the lamb slained, before, or from the foundation of the world.

1st Peter 1:18-20

Verse 18 says that: "…We were not redeemed with corruptible things, as silver and gold, from your vain conversation received by tradition from your fathers; *V19* But with the precious blood of Jesus Christ, as of a lamb without blemish, and without spot. *V20* Who verily was foreordained before the foundation of the world, but was manifest in these last times for you."

Let's look at the word 'foreordained': it means, to designate before hand to a position or functions. In the councils of the triune God, the Lord Jesus, was the Lamb marked out for sacrifice. The word 'foundation' is the translation of a word meaning, literally to throw down, and was used of the laying of the foundation of a house. It speaks of the act of the transcendent God throwing out into space or the universe by speaking the word. The word 'world' in the text is ('kosmos'), which speaks of the creator before the universe was created: The Lord Jesus, has been foreordained to

- THE TRUTH: THE EXTENDED VERSION -

be the savior of lost sinners. The saints, have been foreordained to become recipients of the salvation He would procure, or cause to be in effect for lost sinners at the cross, Ephesians 1:4.

Let's look at one more word, 'Decree' one of the eternal purposes of God, by which events are foreordained. God didn't just look down from heaven and said, oh they don't believe, hell will freeze over before they enter into my rest, No! He made a decree from the foundation of the world, and it's waiting for all who would believe, and if we believe according to scripture His rest is inevitable. When I got saved I didn't know anything about the rest, peace, and the joy of the Lord. I wasn't seeking rest, but I met requirements, and it is so real!

Jesus made a decree that shall stand forever in John 10:9: "I am the door: by me if any Man Enter in, he shall be saved, and shall go in and out, and find pasture." The Greek word 'Sozo' means to deliver or protect, heal, preserve, to make whole: which is the complete rest of God.

LET'S GO A LITTLE DEEPER: REALLY!!?

It amazes me, how a Christian will take another Christian to law, for whatever reason, and if they win the case they praise God for the victory.

But God is not pleased with that kind of behavior. The Spirit of God said through Paul in 1st Corinthians 6:1-4 & 7: "...Dare any of you that have a matter against another, go to law before the unjust, and not before the saints?

V2 Do you not know that the saints will judge the world? And if the world will be judged by you, are you unworthy to judge the smallest matter?

V3 Do you not know that we shall judge angels? How much more things that pertain to this life?

V4 If then you have judgments concerning things pertaining to this life, do you appoint those who are least esteemed in the church to judge?"

- THE TRUTH: THE EXTENDED VERSION -

A very interesting question: "Do you appoint those who are least esteemed in the church."

V5 Then he said: "I say this to your shame. I believe, they that are least esteemed in the church, will show mercy and fairness in a matter." But Paul continues by saying: "...is it so, that there is not a wise man among you, not even one, who will be able to judge between his brethren? *V6* But brother goes to law against brother, and that before the unbelievers.

V7 Now therefore, it is already an utter failure for you that you go to law against one another. Why do you not rather accept wrong? Why do you not rather let yourself be cheated? Nay you yourselves do wrong and cheat, and you do those things to your brethren. So accept the wrong if that be the case, and remember, our Heavenly Father sees all, and knows all, so you can walk away with full confidence, knowing that God have your back!!"

LET'S GO A LITTLE DEEPER: THE OBJECTIVE OF GOD AND SATAN

I was reading the book of Isaiah, Chapter 30 one morning, and the word 'Egypt' stood out. I like doing word studies, because you can gain a lot of insight.

There are four different views of the word 'Egypt' but for the sake of this teaching, I will deal with two of them. The Objective and the Abstract: The word Egypt means: Something hemming in, to surround or enclose.

I was born in the small town of Winnfield, LA, so I'm going to use an example from my youth, to give some clarity to this scenario. My Mother would tell us to catch some of the chickens, and put them in the coop for purification. That was not an easy Job at all, but after a few bruises we got smart. We would throw the food into the corner of the yard, and as they began to eat, we would surround them. That made our Objective; which was to capture them much easier.

We are similar to the chickens, just roaming through life with no purpose, easily devoured. God our Father's objective is to capture

- THE TRUTH: THE EXTENDED VERSION -

us with His unconditional love, His kindness, forgiveness, His grace, mercy and truth.

Troubling as it may be to realize, our adversary the devil, also have an objective; he wants to entangle us with fleshly pleasures. Especially sensual pleasures: Sensual pleasures has the potential to become very ugly. It can be a gateway for debauchery, which means: Excessive indulgence in sensual pleasures.

Look at the way our young lady dresses today: it's all about sensuality. Ladies please hear this: Satan is using a lot of fashion designers to undress our beautiful, and innocent young ladies, and shame on the parents who allow their daughters to dress like that. I'm not talking about adults, I'm talking about kids in their early teens, looking like adults. (I will share more on this in closing).

What's even more disturbing: I'll show you from the word of God how Satan uses the same position: which is a high place, the same method which are words and they both target the simple. It's even recorded in the book of Isaiah. Satan saying "I will be like the Most High". Read Isaiah, Chapter 14 starting with verse 12-17, and see what God our Father, has to say about that!

Let's look at 'Egypt' from an Objective view, it means: a mound of besiegers. The word 'mound' means, an elevation or a high place. The word 'besiegers' means, to surround with armed forces in order to capture. Some of you might agree, that words are the most powerful forces in the world, it depends on how they are used. God our Father wants to use his word, which is the absolute truth: to change our thinking. He wants us to renew our minds with His word, which will deliver us from the blindness we suffered while in unbelief.

- PLEZE RAYBON -

I'm going to give you an insight of 2nd Corinthians 4:3-4: "If our Gospel be hid, it is hid to them that are lost: In whom the god of this world his blinded the minds of them that believe not."

Read this very carefully! We were all unbelievers before coming to Christ, and We were all blinded: and in our state of blindness; we suffered many forms of abuse. This abuse caused us to be rude, and unkind! We suffered many forms of betrayal; which lead to a life of falsehood, arrogance, and on and on. We suffered many ill things in our state of blindness; and in the darkness of his (Satan) hate, we were destined for destruction.

But that scripture continues, saying, "Lest the light of this glorious Gospel of Christ, who is the image of God, should shine unto them." Verse 6 is the kicker, "For God, who commanded the light to shine out of darkness, has shined in our hearts, to give the light of the knowledge of the glory of God in the face of Jesus Christ." So in the light of God's love, we are now destined for eternity with Him.

LET'S GO A LITTLE DEEPER: THE ABSTRACT METHOD OF THE ENEMY

The method I'm about to share with you, literally, no one is exempt! The Truth is all we have, and need to combat this method. So let's start with some definitions.

The word 'Abstract' means: to conceive, or consider, apart from matter. The word 'Conceive' means: to form or develop mentally; plan, devise: to have or form a mental image or idea of. Now it gets more intense! This last definition for the word 'Abstract' is the one that lines up with what I want to share: to become pregnant with. The abstract method derives as a thought, or an idea, and it is for that very reason, the enemy uses this method so effectively, I will repeat, the truth is our weapon of warfare.

We must understand, that we are in direct conflict with unseen entities: something with real, and distinct existence. This is why we are admonished, to be strong in the Lord, and in the power of His might.

How do you do that? Ephesians 6:11 says: you do it by putting on the whole armor of God, and it starts by having your loins girt about with the <u>Truth</u>. He could have said, having your loins girt about with Faith or righteousness. But it is the <u>Truth</u> that activates the breastplate of righteousness, your feet shod with the preparation of the Gospel of peace, the Shield of Faith, the Helmet of Salvation; are all activated by the sword of the Spirit, which is the word of God, the absolute Truth; that you may be able to stand against the wiles, schemes, and plots of the devil.

Here's why this is so important: Ephesians 6:12 says: "we wrestle not against flesh and blood, but we do wrestle against principalities, powers, rulers of the darkness of this world, spiritual wickedness in high places."

What are 'Principalities'? They are rulers in general, particularly angels, and demons, but including earthly magistrates, or rulers.

What are 'magistrates'? Government officers, empowered to administer, and enforce the law.

Spiritual wickedness: denotes the active exercise of a vicious disposition.

Powers: denotes, the power of rule or government, the power of one whose will, and commands must be obeyed by others. This is why we need the Truth to stand against these wiles and schemes of the enemy. As you can see they come in many different forms. Therefore it is vital that we know the Truth. Just being exposed to the Truth is not going to help you stand in the evil day, and we all have them! Jesus said you shall know the Truth, and the Truth will make you free.

Here's my point: you will not be able to use your spiritual authority unless you know the Truth, and you won't know the truth just by

- THE TRUTH: THE EXTENDED VERSION -

reading. – We are instructed to study to show ourselves approved unto God!

I will repeat: this method doesn't have anything to do with the physical realm: it derives as a thought or an idea. This is how James 1:14-15 explains it, and it reveals what the individual has been dwelling on. It says, *V14* "Every man is tempted, when he is drawn away of his own lust, and enticed." His own lust, something he's been dwelling on. *V15* "Then when lust has conceived, it brings forth sin: and sin when it is finished, brings forth death." In order to see this, you must understand that the Spirit of God is identifying lust, as a separate entity from the body, and it reveals how lust or a strong desires, uses the body to bring forth corruption.

Listen closely to this metaphor: most of us understand the process of how a woman conceives a child, sperm and egg connects and conception takes place. Then after a nine month period, this woman is going to bring forth a human, be it boy or girl. In the same way, when lust is conceived; it bring forth sin, and sin; if allowed to run it's full term: brings forth death!

We know thoughts conceived has built entire cities, advanced technology, among many wonderful things. But thoughts conceived has also caused so must pain and sorrow. That's what Paul is referring to: that which brings forth death. Notice how he begins that statement! "Every man is tempted when he is drawn away of his own lust and enticed."

Mark 7:21-22 gives us a full description of what is in man-kind! *V21* "For from within, out of the heart of man proceed: evil thoughts, adulteries, fornications, murders. *V22* Thefts, covetousness, an evil eye, blasphemy, pride, foolishness: all these evil things come

- PLEZE RAYBON -

from within, and defile the man." All of these ills are in the heart or soul of man, and they govern his thoughts. The remedy is in obeying the truth, and it's noticeable. Listen to 1st Peter 1:22-23: "Seeing you have purified your souls in obeying the truth through the Spirit unto unfeigned love of the brethren, see that you love one another with a pure heart fervently: *V23* Being born again, not of corruptible seed, but of incorruptible, by the word of God, which lives and abides forever." Did you get that? I can see that you have purified your souls in obeying the truth. Now that you are capable, love one another with a pure heart.

The soul is the principle of life! Genesis 2:7 says: "God formed man from the dust of the ground, and breathed into his nostrils the breath of life, and man became a living soul." The soul: consisting of the faculties, of thoughts, emotions, and actions, and regarded as a separate entity distinct from the body. Now with that in mind, let me say it this way. Seeing you have purified your thoughts, emotions, and actions in obeying the Truth through the Spirit; see those faculties have to be purified or washed with the truth. Otherwise those thoughts, emotions, and actions will manifest in the physical realm through this abstract method.

I believe this is the primary reason, we are admonished to take control of our thoughts. 1st Peter 1:13: "Therefore gird up the loins of your mind, be sober, and rest your hope fully upon the grace that is to be brought to you at the revelation of Jesus Christ." Philippians 4:8 we are told what to think on, "whatsoever things that are true, honest, just, pure, lovely, and things of a good report. If there be any virtue or praise, think on these things." 2nd Corinthians 10:5: "Casting down imaginations, and every high thing that exalts itself against the knowledge of God, and bringing into captivity every though to the obedience of Christ; and we have the God given power to do that."

- THE TRUTH: THE EXTENDED VERSION -

Here are some things to consider: The <u>mind</u> that has not been renewed typify lust <u>ovaries</u>: it produces or creates thoughts, and images. The <u>imagination</u> typify lust <u>ovulating</u>: it discharges all of those emotions, and feelings of past experiences, and present desires. The <u>enticement</u> typify the <u>sperm</u>. We know a woman doesn't conceive every time she receives the male sperm. Conception can only take place when the sperm and egg connects. Likewise, you don't respond to every enticement. But, when enticement connects with thoughts or Emotions – which typifies the <u>Egg</u> – conception takes place and you will bring forth Corruption.

Let's look at a few scriptures dealing with conceiving. Psalms 7:14: "Behold, he travails with iniquity, and have conceived mischief, and brought forth falsehood." The amplified bible is very blunt, it says "...the wicked man conceives iniquity and is pregnant with mischief and give birth to lies." Job 15:35 says: "They conceived mischief, and bring forth iniquity, and their inmost soul hatches deceit." I will bring more clarity about conceiving in closing. Children of God please understand this, When conception takes place, just resisting is not enough. We are instructed to first submit, and then resist.

39

LET'S GO A LITTLE DEEPER: WHY SUBMIT?

Submitting is the only way out! The word 'submit' means to subordinate: which means, to come under or subject unto the higher powers. Romans 13:1: "Let every soul be subject unto the higher powers. For there is no power but of God: the powers that be are ordained of God." The word 'submit' was originally a Greek military term, meaning to arrange in a military fashion, under the command of a leader. But, in a non-military use, it means a voluntary attitude of giving in, cooperating, assuming responsibility, and carrying a burden.

Submitting will be the harder of the two! Why? Because the individual now has this entity existing inside his soul! It's going to manifest in the physical realm, and it's going to bring forth some form of fleshly pleasures. If you want it to be properly aborted, you should take on the attitude of giving in and cooperate with the word of God. Assume responsibility, and confess that this conception was of your own doing. Then carry the burden for allowing it to cause you to sin. After you've done this, you can resist with confidence.

LET'S GO A LITTLE DEEPER: WHY RESIST?

You resist because Satan doesn't want you to abort his offspring corruption. He's going to do everything in his power to encourage you to bring forth that little ugly thing. If lust is allowed to run its full term or completion, then death is the results! Death of a marriage, death of a ministry, and all the people that are affected, death of trust, death of your name! Please understand this: you don't have to give birth to that little ugly thing called corruption! You can come under the protective hand of God, then of your own will, resist the devil, and he will flee. James 4:7: "But you can't stop there, because lust is still carrying that little ugly thing. You must now confess your sins." 1st John 1:9 says: "If we confess our sins, He is faithful, and just to forgive us our sins, and to cleanse us from all unrighteousness." God will cleanse you, and stop lust from giving birth to corruption.

But He is clearly saying in Chapter 2, Verse 1 & 2, don't abuse my mercy, saying, "My little children, these things write I unto you, that you sin not. And if any man sin, we have an advocate with the Father, Jesus Christ the righteous: And He is the propitiation for our sins, and not for ours only, but also for the sins of the whole world."

- PLEZE RAYBON -

Because of Adam: The whole world needs a Savior, and Jesus is the Propitiation or Atonement for our redemption, the act of delivering from sin or saving from evil.

LET GO A LITTLE DEEPER: INORDINATE AFFECTION.

Earlier I used the term, bringing forth, so give this topic your undivided attention! I want to show you the effects caused by abuse. Let's look at the words 'Inordinate Affection', these words primarily denotes whatever one experiences in anyway, which affects him hence, an affection of the mind; which stimulates a passionate desire, or capricious delight. The disease of passion, always used in a bad sense: it primarily denotes, whatever one suffers or experiences.

I do understand that mental illness is real. But, a lot of what we are seeing, is not mental illness, its 'Inordinate Affection' brought on by physical, or mental abuse.

After many studies, and observations they found that most serial killers, where abused as a child. Earlier in the book we defined the word 'conceived', and one of the definitions means: to develop mentally. When you abuse a child, you are stimulating a passionate desire; that will develop into a disease of passion. We are seeing these mass killings, and saying how can someone be so heartless to do something like that?

That is the effects of 'Inordinate Affections', and they were not born that way, they developed into that through a channel called abuse. We are warned in Ephesians 6:4: "provoke not your children to wrath; but bring them up in the nurture and admonition of the Lord." Colossians 3:21 reveals the danger of violating this scripture. "Fathers, Provoke not your children to anger, lest they become <u>Discouraged</u>."

Let's look at some more definitions, which will give us a better understanding. The word discouraged, in the Greek means: Athumeo, it means, to be 'Disheartened' or 'Dispirited'. 'Disheartened' means: to lose hope, depressed, discouraged. The B part of Ephesians 6:4 says: "but bring them up in the fear and admonition of the Lord." Scripture is very clear on this issue.

Proverbs 22:6 says: "Train up a child in the way he should go, and when he is old, he will not depart from it." I know many of you know this scripture by memory, but have you ever meditated on that scripture? The definition took me for a Spin! The word 'train' in the text means: to <u>narrow</u>. I'm going to give this scripture first, and then my point of view. Matthew 7:13-14: "Enter in by the <u>narrow</u> gate; for wide is the gate, and broad is the way that leads to destruction, and there are many who go in by it. *V14* Because <u>narrow</u> is the gate and difficult is the way which leads to life, and there are few who find it."

When you are training a child, you are <u>narrowing</u> his options. While in training he's learning this is wrong, and will never be accepted, or this is right, and will always be approved. What are you doing? You are making a straight path to life, and when he or she is old they won't depart from it. There's a catch to it: it must be done by example. You can't say, do as I say, and not as I do; that will not go over too well.

- THE TRUTH: THE EXTENDED VERSION -

I remember my dad smoking a cigarette, saying, I better not ever catch y'all with one of these in your mouth. So we made sure he didn't catch us, we would steal a few and go play in woods and smoke. Children don't need to be confused while developing, like a lot of us were!

LET'S GO A LITTLE DEEPER: PROVERBS 6:16 THESE SIX THINGS GOD HATES AND SEVEN IS AN ABOMINATION.

The first of these is a proud look: Psalms 101:5: "Him that has a high look and a proud heart will I not suffer." Psalms 138:6: "Though the Lord is high, yet hath he respect unto the lowly but the proud He knows afar off." Proverbs 16:5: "Every one that is proud is an abomination to the Lord: though hand, join in hand, he shall not go unpunished.

There are many examples in the word of God: Let's take a look at King Uzziah in 2nd Chronicles 26:15-21. Please read the whole story starting in verse one.

Uzziah became King at the age of sixteen, and He reigned fifty two years, and he did what was right in the sight of God. He had 2,000 mighty men of valor, and under their hands, was an army of 307,500 that help the king against the enemy. The last part of verse 15 says: "...his fame spread far abroad; for he was marvelously helped, till he was strong. ^{V16} But when he was strong, his heart was lifted up to his destruction: for He

- THE TRUTH: THE EXTENDED VERSION -

transgressed against the Lord his God, and went into the temple of the Lord to burn incense upon the Alter of incense. *V17* Azariah the Priest took eighty Priests of the Lord, man of courage."

V18 They opposed King Uzziah, "saying it is not for you, Uzziah to burn incense to the Lord. The sons of Aaron are consecrated to burn incense; and told him to get out of the sanctuary; because you have trespassed, and that will not be to your honor before the Lord God." *V19* "Uzziah became very angry and had a Censer in his hand to burn incense. While he was angry with the Priest the leprosy broke out on his forehead." Uzziah was a leper until the day of his death. I repeat Proverbs 16:5: "every one that is proud, is an abomination to the Lord, though hand join in hand, he shall not go unpunished."

LET'S GO A LITTLE DEEPER: A LYING TONGUE, AND HANDS THAT SHED INNOCENT BLOOD

I'm going to put these next two points together, because this next story reveals the detriment of lying.

Psalms 63:11: "The king shall rejoice in God; every one that swears by him shall glory: but the mouth of them that speak lies shall be stopped." Proverbs 19:5: "A false witness shall not be unpunished, and he that speaks lies shall not escape."

Revelation 21:8 says: "The fearful, unbelieving, the abominable, murderers, whoremongers, sorcerers, idolaters, and all liars shall have their part in the lake which burns with fire, and brimstone: which is the second death."

There is a fascinating story in 1st Kings 21, through chapter 22. (Please read the whole story).

Naboth the Jezreelite had a vineyard which was in Jezreel, next to the Palace of Ahab King of Samaria. Ahab asked Naboth to give

- THE TRUTH: THE EXTENDED VERSION -

him his vineyard, because it was near his home: and he wanted to grow vegetables in it. He offered to give him a better one, or give him the wroth in money.

V3 "Naboth said to Ahab, the Lord forbid that I should give the inheritance of my father unto you."

Ahab was very displeased with his answer. *V5* Jezebel his wife came to him, and said: "why is your spirit so sad, and you eat no bread?" Ahab said: "because Naboth won't give me the vineyard."

V7 Jezebel said to him: "do you not govern Israel? Arise and eat bread, and let your heart be happy. I will give you the vineyard of Naboth the Jezreelite." *V8* She fabricated a lie against Naboth by writing letters in Ahab's name, and sealed them with his seal, and sent them to the elders and nobles who dwelt with Naboth in his city. *V9* In the letters she said, "proclaim a fast, and set Naboth on high among the people." *V13* and set two men, sons of Belial, before him, to bear witness against him Saying, "you did blasphemed God, and the king."

Then he was carried out of the city, and stoned to death. Naboth life was taken because of that lie.

But God is faithful to fulfill his word. *V16* When Ahab heard that Naboth was dead: Ahab rose up to go to the vineyard of Naboth the Jezreelite, to take possession of it.

V17 "The word of the Lord came to Elijah the Tish'bite, saying, *V18* "Arise, go down to meet Ahab King of Israel, in Samaria. He is in the vineyard of Naboth, where he is gone to possess it." *V19* say to him, "thus says the Lord: Have you killed and also taken possession? "Thus says the Lord, in the place where dogs lick

- PLEZE RAYBON -

the blood of Naboth shall lick your blood, even yours." *V20* Ahab replied: "have you found me oh my enemy?" Elijah answered, "I have found you, because you have sold yourself to do evil in the sight of the Lord. See says the Lord, I will bring evil on you and utterly sweep away and cut off from Ahab every male bond and free." (You will find the fulfillment of that in 2nd Kings 10.)

1st Kings 22:1: "...Now Syria and Israel continued without war for three years. *V2* In the third year Jehoshaphat King of Judah went down to meet Ahab King of Israel. *V3* Ahab said to him: do you know that Ramoth in Gilead is ours. And we keep silence and do not take it from the King of Syria?

V4 Then He asked him, will you go with me to Ramoth Gilead to battle? *V5* Jehoshaphat said I am as you are, my people as your people, my horses as your horses. But inquire first I pray you, for the word of the Lord <u>Today</u>.

V6 Ahab gathered together 400 Prophets, all of whom agreed with him. *V7* "Jehoshaphat said is there another Prophet of the Lord here whom we may ask?" *V8* "Ahab said yes, there's one more man, Micaiah son of Imlah, by whom we may inquire of the Lord, but I hate him, Because he never prophesy good concerning me, but evil. Jehoshaphat said, let not the king say that.

V13 The messenger who went to call Micaiah said to him. "Behold now, the Prophets unanimously declare good to the King. Let your answer, I pray you be like theirs, and say what is good." But Micaiah said, "I will speak what the Lord says to me."

V15 He took him to the King, and the King asked him, "shall we go against Ramoth Gilead to battle or hold back?" Micaiah said, "go and proper, for the Lord will deliver it into the king's hand."

- THE TRUTH: THE EXTENDED VERSION -

V16 Then Ahab said "how many times, must I charge you to tell me nothing but the truth in the name of the Lord?" Now please get this: King Ahab asked for the truth, but listen to his response to it.

V17 Micaiah gives him the truth: "saying I saw all Israel scattered upon the hills as sheep that had no Shepherd, and the Lord said, these have no master. Let them return every man to his house in peace.

V18 Ahab said to Jehoshaphat, "did I not tell you that he would prophesy no good concerning me, but evil?" *V19* Micaiah said, hear the word of the Lord: (Now you will get a glimpse of how our Heavenly Father operates). "I saw the Lord sitting on His throne, and all the host of heaven standing by him on his right hand, and on the left.

V20 Then the Lord said, Who will I send to persuade Ahab to go up and fall at Ramoth-gilead? One said on this manner, and one said on that manner." *V21* Then there came forth a spirit, and stood before the Lord, and said, "I will persuade him." *V22* The Lord said unto him, "how are you going to it?" He said, "I will go forth, and I will be a Lying Spirit in the mouth of all his prophets." And He (The Lord) said, "you shall persuade him, and prevail also, go forth, and do so."

Please read the rest of that chapter so you can see Ahab's fall. But this is what I want you to see: His wife Jezebel, fabricated lies which took a man's life, and God used a lying spirit, to take her husband Ahab's life. Proverbs 6:16 the second, of the six things God hates, is A lying tongue, and third one He hates, is Hands that shed innocent blood! He did both of them.

- PLEZE RAYBON -

The 4th thing God hates, A heart that devise wicked imaginations.

Roman 1:21: "When they knew God, they glorified him not as God, neither were thankful; but became vain in their imaginations, and their foolish heart was darkened."

The 5th thing God hates, "Feet that is swift in running to mischief."

Proverbs 4:16: "For they sleep not, except they have done mischief: and their sleep is taken away, unless they cause someone to fall."

The 6 thing God hates, A false witness that speak lies.

Proverbs 12:17: "He that speaks the truth shows forth righteousness: but a false witness deceit." Proverbs 19:9: "A false witness shall not be unpunished, and he that speaks lies shall perish."

This 7th one, 'Sowing Discord' among brethren, is an abomination to God. What is an abomination? Something disgusting.

The Hebrew word <u>Toebah</u> defines it as something or someone, essentially unique in the sense of being dangerous, sinister, and repulsive to another individual. When used with reference to God, this word describes people, things, acts, relationships, and characteristics, that are detestable to him, because they are contrary to His nature: such things that relates to death and idolatry. Here is a warning from Job 4:8: "Even as I have seen, they that plow iniquity, and sow wickedness, reap the same." Proverbs 6:14: "<u>Frowardness</u> is in his heart, he devise mischief continually; he sows discord."

LET'S GO A LITTLE DEEPER: WHAT IS SATAN REALLY AFTER? Faith & Love!

If you are thinking that Satan's only objective, is to get you to sin, then you are sadly mistaken. I even hear people say, he wants to steal your testimony. That might be true, but he has his sight on something that will cause your testimony to be hampered. A large percentage of the Body of Christ doesn't have a clue to what he is after!

There are two major fruit Satan wants to pillage – Faith and Love, and here are the primary reasons. Satan knows that the armor of faith, is the only thing that can quench all his fiery darts. Ephesians 6:16: "above all, taking the shield of Faith, wherewith you shall be able to quench all the fiery darts of the wicked."

He also knows that without Faith it is impossible to please God. Hebrews 11:6: "Without Faith it is impossible to please God: He that comes to God, must believe that He is, and that He is a <u>Rewarder</u> of them that diligently seek Him."

Secondly, he wants to keep us from walking in genuine love. Why? Because Faith works by Love! The last part of Galatians

- PLEZE RAYBON -

5:6 Paul says: "that in Christ the only thing that is of value or worth, is Faith, which works by love."

I'm going to give you another metaphor: let me clarify, this is a metaphor, not a new teaching on faith.

I observed something at a 'word of faith' church one Sunday, and it put me on a search for answers. This is what I observed: The church had a guest speaker that day, and before he finished speaking he stated: if there's anyone in here being tormented by a spirit of fear, come forward and I will pray for you, and over half the church went up for prayer.

I thank God for that brother being sensitive to the spirit, and the people that were honest enough to respond. But, according to the word of God, something was desperately wrong with that picture.

2nd Timothy 1:7 says: "God has not given us a spirit of fear, but of power, love, and of a sound mind". Jesus addressed the issue concerning fear in Matthew 6:30, 8:26, and 16:18. In each case he ended his statement with the phrase, "Oh ye of little Faith." Two places in particular, "why are you fearful, oh ye of little faith?" "Why did you doubt, oh ye of little of faith?" That tells me that fear and doubting are a result of little or a lack of faith! Read Revelations 21:8 again, to see the category God places fear in, and read Isaiah 8:13, you will see that it offends Him (God), when we walk in fear, or not trusting Him.

The word 'little faith' in those two verses means a lack of confidence in Christ. We need to consider something here. Why? Because this took place, in a so called 'Word of Faith' Church! The Pastor is an excellent teacher: so what's the problem?

- THE TRUTH: THE EXTENDED VERSION -

Maybe it's that, faith is more than something you use to try and get things from God. That's what 'faith' seems to be, in a lot of those churches. They have their little books of confessions, and their confessions are centered on getting things, which has nothing to do with faith.

Scripture is very clear, on how to get things! Matthew 6:33: "you seek first the Kingdom of God, and His righteousness; and all these things will be added unto you." These things are added as you mature in the things of God! I hope this metaphor will bring some clarity to what faith is and how it comes to us. It was obvious the people hadn't got it: the proof was at the altar. I will repeat,this is a metaphor, not a new doctrine on faith.

For those of you that might say, I never really understood what a metaphor is, here's the definition: A figure of speech in which one object: or idea is compared, or identified with another, in order to suggest, a similarity between the two.

I was reading Romans 12, which I had read many times, but this time I couldn't get past the third verse. The last part of that verse reads, "according as God has dealt to every man the <u>measure</u> of <u>faith</u>."

The way that passage is phrased, it reminded me of another passage I had read. As I sat there staring at the verse, the Spirit of God gave me a reference, which took me to Genesis 2:7, it says: "And the Lord God formed man of the dust of the ground, and breathed into his nostrils the <u>breath</u> of <u>life</u>, and he became a living soul."

As I began to ponder that, I began saying it over and over to myself, "the breath of life, the measure of faith". That's when I saw the similarity.

When you were born physically, you received the breath of life, and at that very moment, God put two things in operation that will sustain you for a life time: Breathing and the heart-beat, they go hand in hand. Breathing causes the heart to beat which keeps the blood flowing, to nourish the trillions of cells in the body, and no one needs to teach you how to Breath. As long as you keep the body nourished, breathing won't be a problem, and as you grow physically, the capacity for oxygen increases. It's a natural occurrence! It's important to know, that the breath of life was given by God our Father.

In the same manner: when you were born again spiritually, you received the measure of Faith, and at that very moment, God put two things in operation, that will sustain your spiritual life which will never end. These are Faith and Love: They go hand in hand! Faith is the oxygen, and Love is the Heart-beat, and as you grow spiritually; the capacity for Faith and Love increases, it's a spiritual occurrence! It is equally important to know that the measure of faith, was given by God the Father, and only He can cause it to increase as you grow in Him.

Just as the breath of life supports the physical body to do the many things it's able to do, based on the gifts and talents given by God. Romans 12:3 Reveals to us that God gave the measure or the proportion of faith to support the spiritual gifts, that are mentioned in verses 6-8, and the many facets of those gifts. I hope through that metaphor you were able to see that faith is more than just a life style or something you use to get things. It is the very oxygen that supports our spiritual life: without it we die.

- THE TRUTH: THE EXTENDED VERSION -

What I saw was very disturbing!! These churches are filled every Sunday, and faith is the primary subject. So why is the altar filled with over half the church tormented by a spirit of fear? There may be other reasons, but this one is obvious according to scripture. 'A lack of love'!!!

1st John 4:18: "There is no fear in love: but perfect love casts out fear; because fear has torment. He that fears is not made perfect in love." I will repeat Galatians 5:6, this is the kicker. The last part of that verse says "faith works by love". This is the primary reason faith is not active in the lives of many, because they are not walking in genuine love toward the brethren. 1st Peter 1:22 talks about having "unfeigned love for the brethren..." which means: not <u>pretend</u> or <u>hypocritical</u> but <u>Genuine</u>, <u>Sincere</u> love for one another.

I made a statement earlier about how everything you've ever experienced is lodged in the soul. Think about it, a life time of good and bad experiences. If the soul is not purified, by obeying the Truth through the Spirit, you won't be able to love genuinely, you won't allow yourself to be vulnerable. There's always a wall to protect your emotions. I hope you can see that you can't have genuine love, without being vulnerable. When genuine love is in operation: there's always a chance of getting hurt or wounded, Jesus was and is our example.

Just as the heart can't function without breathing, faith can't function without love. Habakkuk 2:4: "The just shall 'Live' by Faith." Just as the physical body lives by breathing, your Spiritual body lives by Faith! Faith is your spiritual breath of life. As you grow and mature in the things of God through obeying the truth: the soul is being purified, and the unfeigned love of God fills your heart.

- PLEZE RAYBON -

If the soul is not being purified, through obeying the truth: then genuine love lies dormant, and if genuine love lies dormant, faith can not increase. It's like having asthma: you can Breathe, but not fully. But you need your Faith to increase! In order for that to take place: genuine love is paramount to cast out all fear.

Genuine love is only acquired, through the purifying of the soul in obeying the Truth. This will allow the Spirit of God to pour the light of his love, into all of those dark places; enabling you to breathe fully, Spiritually.

A co-worker of mine was rushed to the hospital with a congested heart. When he returned to work, I asked him: what were the symptoms? His answer was: I couldn't Breathe! That gives this metaphor more validity. Hopefully you can see why Satan, our adversary, wants to pillage these two major fruits. Notice I said pillage, because when a large amount of something is taken, you notice it right away. But when real small portions are taken, you won't notice it until it's too late. Your adversary the devil, has been pillaging your Love walk. Without love, Faith automatically fails.

LET'S GO A LITTLE DEEPER: THE MISCONCEPTION OF FAITH.

God didn't put this life giving force called Faith, in the hands of man. Why? Because God knew man would exploit it, just as he has done, under the guise of a so called movement of God. Yes! The movement had it's positives, it made people realize: The just shall live by Faith, and made people like myself really study the word!

Then it became commercialized: People jumping on board for financial gain; which brought on board those who didn't know what they were talking about, saying, "We walk by Faith and not by sight." Then they would say: Peter began to sink, when he took his eyes off Jesus. When Jesus Himself, told us why he began to sink, saying, "Why did you doubt? It had nothing to do with him taking his eyes off Jesus; he leaned to his own understanding: like many of us do!

I'm going to give you a scripture first, then I'm going to share with you the misconception of faith.

If you are a believer I want you to know that this scripture is speaking directly to you. St. John 1:12-13: "But as many as received Him, to

- PLEZE RAYBON -

them He gave power to become the sons of God, even to them that believe on his name:" Now please give close attention to verse 13: "Which were born not of blood, nor of the will of the flesh, nor of the will of man, 'BUT OF GOD'.

It was God who breathed the initial breath of life into man and it is God who dealt to man the measure of faith: and He's the only one who can increase your Faith. I heard this one pastor say, faith is like a muscle, the more you use it the bigger it gets. That statement has no scriptural support!

My question is, how do you use Faith? The Greek word 'Pistis' is used more than any word for faith in the Bible. It means: a firm persuasion, a conviction based upon hearing. It's always used of Faith in God, Christ, or Spiritual things.

My point is: you won't find Faith in a book of confessions. Remember this was a so called 'Word of Faith' Church, and they are steeped in confessions. But yet the altar was filled with over half the church, tormented by a spirit of fear. I must add, faith is not positive thinking; but as you grow in God you will have a positive outlook on life!

Let me share something else with you that might shock you. A large percentage of the Body of Christ, are led to believe that faith comes by reading their bible and coming to church to hear the word preached. This is not so, although both are desperately essential. The sad part is they don't realize it until they are being attacked by the enemy. 2nd Timothy 3:16 show's us the limitations of the word of God which is extremely vast, but yet limited. Listen closely as you read! "All scripture is given by inspiration of God, and is profitable for doctrine, reproof, correction, and for instruction in righteousness.

- THE TRUTH: THE EXTENDED VERSION -

V17 "That the man of God maybe perfect (or mature), thoroughly furnished unto all good works." But it won't produce faith!

This is why it is so important to have a vibrant and intimate relationship with God the Holy Spirit, because without it the bible is just another book. A very interesting book; that will benefit you immensely! But according to 1st Corinthians 2:14 "The things of God are spiritually discerned," and again it's limited. Here's why: there are two Greek definitions for word, 'Logos' and 'Rhema'.

The 'Logos' is the written or spoken word of God, and according to John 1:14: His word became flesh and dwelt among us: (Jesus) is the Logos personified, and He came to save us and to teach us kingdom principles, and to inspire us to seek the living God, not a religion. Thank about this: the disciples walked with the 'Logos' (Jesus) every day, but they didn't study Him. They observed Him, and were amazed at what He was doing, saying, what manner of man is this? – even the wind, and the waves obey Him.

I want you to see what took place after feeding the 5,000 in Matthew 14:21 and then the 4,000 in Matthew 15:38. After being part of those miracles, Matthew 16:5-12 will explain what I'm referring to: "when the disciples reached the other side of the sea, found that they had forgot to bring bread." Jesus began to teach them about the leaven of the Pharisees and Sadducees. These knuckleheads thought He was talking about bread. Jesus being aware of what they were saying, asked, why are you discussing among yourselves the fact that you have no bread, oh you man of little faith. In verse 9, you can feel the tone of frustration: "Do you not yet discern, or understand? Do you not remember the five loaves of the five thousand, and how many baskets you gathered? What about the seven loaves for the four thousand, and how many baskets you took

- PLEZE RAYBON -

up? How is it that you fail to understand that I was not talking about bread? *V12* "Then they understood."

Please understand this, the 'Logos' is an ocean of information about our Father: revealing His love and kindness, what pleases Him, and what is not pleasing to Him. It will benefit us by way of reproof, rebuke or correction, and for instruction in righteousness that we may be perfect or mature. I want to draw your attention to the word 'may' because this word is used in some cases to express possibilities or power to do. My point is you may or may not mature in the things of God. I know that to be true in the lives of many. They have been exposed to the 'Logos' for years, but never came to a play of maturity! I'm aware that it takes time to come to that place, but that statement still stands true. Here is the purpose of the 'Logos', it's to make you perfect or mature, 'Complete'.

This is exactly what Hebrews 4:12 is indicating, "For the 'Logos' or written word of God is Quick, and Powerful, and sharper than any two edged sword, piercing even to the dividing asunder of soul and spirit, and of the joints and marrow, and is a discerner of the thoughts and intents of the heart." The 'Logos' primary purpose is for us to learn the ways of God; and to make us aware of the things that will hinder our Spiritual growth, and it is the prerequisite for 'Rhema'. In case you don't know the definition of 'prerequisite', here it is: a thing that is required as a prior condition for something else to happen or exist. Now that you see something is required of you, for something else to happen: Then you prepare yourself by studying to show yourself approved unto God! When you study, you don't pass words you don't understand. No, you make sure you know and understand what the 'Logos' is revealing.

Here are the benefits of storing the 'Logos' in your heart: This is where ('Rhema') is revealed. God the Holy Spirit is going to take

- THE TRUTH: THE EXTENDED VERSION -

the scriptures that you have stored in your heart, and use them as a tool to help you in times of need. Psalm 46:1: God is our refuge and strength, a very present help in time of need. To speak a 'Rhema' word to help you: to open the eyes of your understanding.

Referring back to Matthew 16:13-18, here you will see the Logos and the Rhema on disply; when Jesus ask His disciples, who do men say that the Son of man am? They gave Him the Logos, that what was written or said, saying some say you are John the Baptist, some say Elijah, and others say, you are Jeremiah or one of the Prophets. Then Jesus said, but who do you say that I am? Peter received a Rhema word from God saying, you are the Christ: The Son of the living GOD. Jesus response said it all, saying to him, flesh and blood did not reveal that to you, But my Father which is in heaven.

Then Jesus said something so fascinating, He said Peter on that Rock we are going to build our Church. What was that Rock? It was an utterance from GOD, and that's what God is building His Church on, a Rhems word. 1st Peter 2:5: we are as living stones being built up into a spiritual house, an holy priesthood, to offer up spiritual sacrifices... It's through those experiences you will encounter through your obedience, that your faith will Increases! Romans 10:17 says, Faith comes by hearing and hearing by the word (or 'Rhema') of God. It's Preparation: 'Rhema' is not a given, it's seeking Him and submitting to His word that you might find the fullness of HIM. Maybe you can see it this way: The Father gave us the (Logos) to learn of Him. Then God looks for someone who has learned of Him, and is faithful and obedient. Then God the Holy Spirit will speak a Rhema word, whicn is an <u>utterane</u> from God, and it's never for the individual, although he will benefit from it, but it's alway for the advancement of the Kingdom of God, and we are all blessed because of someones obedience.

- PLEZE RAYBON -

Earlier I made a statement that in Genesis, you will see the first of everything. I know that 'Rhema' is a greek definition for word. The Hebrew word is 'Dabar' and it has the same significance as does Rhema. When you look at Genesis, Chapter 6:5-8: "When the Lord saw that the wickedness of man was great in the earth, and that every imagination of his heart were only evil continually. It grieved Him (God), to his heart that He even made man." *V7* "God said I will destroy man whom I have created from the face of the earth." God was going to kill everything He had created. *V8* But Noah found favor in the eyes of the Lord. (Question)–Did God just find favor or (grace) in Noah; or was it something that was said? Here is the answer: yes it was something that was said, and you will know that it was a work of the Holy Spirit based on the results.

Genesis 5:28: When Lamech was 182 years old he had a son and named him Noah, saying, "This one shall bring us relief and comfort from our work and toil of our hands due to the ground being cursed by God. See how that works? You must understand this: God will not do anything on earth apart from man. When you understand Psalms 115:16, It says: "The heavens belong to the Lord, but He has given the earth to the children of man." For instance, you give someone a car as a gift: now, just because you gave it to him or her, it doesn't mean you can grab the keys, and take off without their permission.

That's how our Father is toward us, when God wants to do something in the earth, He will speak a word to a Faithful servant; for him to speak and act on. Our Father God gave us acess; to give Him entrance into our affairs. So study the 'logos' and allow it to cause a maturity; that will cause your faith to be unmovable, and always abounding in the things of God, enabling you to encourage others. Here is the good news: God wants to speak to all of us in a clear and personal way, and He's not hiding, he's waiting for your maturity!

LET'S GO A LITTLE DEEPER: UNSHAKABLE FAITH OF NOAH AND ABRAHAM.

There are many Patriarchs in the Bible, but let's focus on two of them: Noah and Abraham. Let's see what motivated them, to stand firm when faced with impossible odds. Hebrews 11:7: "Noah being warned of God of things not seen as yet, moved with fear, prepared an ark to the saving of his house; by the which he condemned the world, and became heir of the righteousness which is by faith." Genesis 5:32: "Noah was five hundred years old." Genesis 6:8 says: "He found grace in the eyes of the Lord in spite of all the wickedness and violence he was surrounded by." Genesis 6:13: "God said unto Noah, the end of all flesh is come before me; because the earth is filled with violence through them; and, behold, I will destroy them with the earth." The Hebrew word for 'said' is 'Amar' this word refers to the simple act of communicating with the spoken word. It can be used of direct or indirect speech as well. But when used by God it's more than making a statement: It's authoritative, usually with a command or instruction. Genesis 6:14-15: "God told him to build an ark, and gave him the dimensions on how to build it." Genesis 6:17: "God told him how He was going to destroy and kill every living thing on the face of the earth." Genesis 6:18-22: "But with thee will I establish my covenant; you and your family shall come into the ark." God instructed him to take two of every kind of living things, male and female, from cattle to creeping things. He told him to gather food for himself, and for the animals. What a task! But we read that Noah did according to all that God commanded him, so did He.

A hundred years later when Noah was six hundred, God told him in the 7th chapter of Genesis, verse 4: "in seven days I will cause it to rain for forty days and forty nights." Now think for a moment how Noah must have felt after being criticized daily. You know they mocked him, called him crazy, but he continued to obey God, and now it's about to pay off. Genesis 7:6 says: "Noah was six hundred when the floods of water was upon the earth." *V11* "In the six hundredth year of Noah's life, the second month, the seventeenth day of the month, the same day were all the fountains of the great deep were broken up, and the windows of heaven were opened." *V13* "...Noah and his family went into the ark." *V16* "...and they went in male and female of all flesh, as God had commanded him: and the Lord shut them in."

Noah was able to stand firm, in the face of opposition, because God spoke to him personally, and he believed God, and Obeyed. Because of his obedience; God blessed him, and his family. You don't get this kind of confidence from listening to man. He can only give you the inspired word, and it should inspire you to seek the living God. Whom, will cause you to experience Isaiah 40:31. This is from the Amplified Bible: But those who wait for the Lord [who expect, look for, and hope in Him] shall change, and renew their strength, and power; they shall lift their wings, and mount up [close to God] as eagles [mount up to the sun]; they shall run, and not be weary, they shall walk, and not faint,

- THE TRUTH: THE EXTENDED VERSION -

or become tired. That's what Noah experienced from waiting on the Lord!

ABRAHAM

Let's look at the man Abraham, formerly known as Abram. After reading his story, all I can say is wow!! You can see why they called him the father of Faith. It would take too much time to cover everything about Abraham, but read Genesis, Chapters 15 through 21:1-18, and be amazed again at the awesomeness of God. I'm going to focus on the revelation the Holy Spirit gave us through Paul in Romans 4. Then we will talk about some of the things revealed in Genesis.

Romans 4:18: "Who against hope believed in hope, that he might become the Father of many nations, according to that which was spoken, so shall thy seed be. *V19* Being not weak in faith, he considered not his own body now dead, when he was about a hundred years old, neither the deadness of Sarah's womb. *V20* He staggered not at the promises of God through unbelief, but was strong in faith giving glory to GOD; *V21* and being fully persuaded that what He had promised, He was able also to perform." I'm going to come back to this later!

Genesis 16:16, reveals to us that Abram was 86 years old when he had a son, by his hand maid Hager. Thirteen years later, In Genesis 17:1, when he was 99, <u>God</u> talked with him. *V5* God changed his name to Abraham. *V7* God said to Abraham, "I will establish my covenant between me and you, and thy seed after you, in their generation for an everlasting covenant, to be a God unto you, and thy seed after you."

- PLEZE RAYBON -

Genesis 17:10, God explained to him the terms of the covenant, "that every male child among you shall be circumcised." *V11* "And you shall circumcise thy foreskin; and it will be a token of the covenant between me and you." Then in verses 15-16, God said to Abraham, "as for Sarai thy wife, thou shall not call her name Sarai, but Sarah shall her name be called. *V16* And I will bless her, and give thee a son also of her." I always hear people talk about how Sarah laughed, but when you read verse 17. Abraham fell upon his face and laughed, and said in his heart, "shall a child be born unto him that is a hundred years old, and Sarah that is ninety years old bear?"

It's been said that Abraham didn't doubt God, and they base it on that statement in Romans 4:20, where it says: "He staggered not at the promises of God through unbelief; but was strong in Faith, giving glory to God." But in Genesis 17:17, He seems to have questions, which can sound doubtful, in verse 18, "and Abraham said to God, Oh that Ishmael might live before thee!" It might seem like that statement had little, or no significance. But it was totally legitimate, because in their culture the inheritance always went to the first born. But God said "no, thy wife Sarah shall bear thee a son."

Personally I believe he doubted at first! (Notice I said personally) because it's my opinion, meaning you can receive it or not. When you know someone and establish a relationship, everything changes; your Heart just knows, and Abraham came to know that He is a God that cannot lie. This is the promise I believe the Holy Spirit is referring to in Romans 4:20-21 where it says: "Abraham staggered not at the promises of God through unbelief, but was strong in faith giving glory to God, and being fully persuaded." Which would or should indicate he was not fully persuaded at

- THE TRUTH: THE EXTENDED VERSION -

first. But understanding who God is, he knew what God had promised He was also able to perform!

Abraham believed God! How do I know that? In Genesis 17:23 it says: "Abraham took Ishmael his son, and every male among the men in his house, even the ones that were bought, and circumcised them, *V24* and Abraham was ninety nine years old, when he was circumcised." You know the rest of the story: God visited Sarah as He had promised. Sarah conceived and bore Abraham a son in his old age, at the set time of which God had spoken to him, and Abraham was a hundred years old.

It was hearing God speak to him personally; that produced that kind of faith, or confidence in God. Earlier in the book I expressed the difference between the (Logos & Rhema), which are New Testament or Greek definitions. Noah and Abraham are Old Testament individuals. I looked at the Hebrew word 'Dabar' which has many applications, and it expressed the same significance as does 'Rhema'. I believe that's why the Holy Spirit referenced them in the New Testament. It indicates there's no difference, when God speaks to an individual, and the individual obeys, and sees the results: It produces Unshakable faith. I could show you many more Phenomenon's of Faith, and they are all based on God speaking to the individual, and not the Individual approaching God, with a book of confessions or positive thinking.

The Spirit of God is still speaking to his people today. When you prepare yourself to hear the Spirit of God speak to you, by studying to show yourself approved unto Him. Purifying the soul through obeying the truth unto unfeigned love of the Brethren, which means, to have a genuine love for the Brethren! Be transformed by the renewing of the mind. Then take control of your thoughts by thinking on whatsoever things that are true, honest, just, pure,

- PLEZE RAYBON -

lovely, and of a good report. Submit yourself to God, and resist the demands of the flesh. Instead of bringing forth corruption, you will bring forth that what is good, and acceptable, and perfect will of God. So walk as Children of light; to bring forth fruit unto Eternal Life by putting on the Breastplate of Faith and Love, and for a Helmet: THE HOPE OF SALVATION. HALLELUJAH!!!

IN CLOSING: THE JUDGEMENT

Let's go back to the judgement: Genesis 3:15, God said some things in that verse, that shouldn't be over looked. God said to Satan, after he deceived the woman saying: "I will put enmity between you and the woman, and between your seed or (offspring) and between her seed; or (offspring)." I want you to see that Satan has seed or offspring in the earth. We see in Romans 5:12: "By one man sin entered into the world, but sin had a tag-along that dominated, called death, so death passed upon all men, for or because of that, all have sinned. Verse 14 says: death reigned even over them that had not sinned after similitude of Adam transgression. Meaning: We didn't do what they did; so how did it trickle down to us?

I have heard a few statements, but with no specifics; which can leave a gray area in the mind. Some say, it's because Adam was the representative of man-kind, true statement, but no specifics. Some say, through procreation, very true statement, but no specifics. But the word of God is specific: Acts 17:26 says: "He has made of one <u>blood</u>, all nations of men for to dwell on all the face of the earth." <u>One Blood</u>, and here is the Truth! There is a speck of blood in the sperm of the male, and that speck of blood

- PLEZE RAYBON -

is what causes sin and death to be replicated. That is exactly why Jesus was born not of blood, nor of the will of men, but of God. The blood line starts with the man.

I asked google, saying, "is there blood in the sperm of the male?" (google answer): "it is common to see blood in the semen of the male". That wasn't the answer I was looking for! So I asked where does the embryo get it's blood from. (Cha-ching), it says: "the embryo starts with it's own blood". My response was 'YEAH' that speck of blood that comes from the male. So scripture tells us in 1st Corinthians 15:22: "For as in Adam all die, even so in Christ shall all be made alive."

Here is my point: if you have not accepted Jesus Christ as your Lord and savior: you are still dead in trespasses and sins, and you are Satan's offspring. Paul explains it like this: Ephesians 2:1-5: "And you He made alive, when you were dead in trespasses and sins. *V2* In which you once walked according to the course of this world, according to prince of the power of the air, the spirit who now works in the children of disobedience. *V3* Among whom also we all once conducted ourselves in the lusts of our flesh, fulfilling the desires of the flesh, and of the mind, and were by nature the children of God's wrath just like everyone else.

V4 But God, who is rich in mercy, because of His great love with which He loved us. *V5* Even when we were dead by (our own) shortcomings and trespasses. He made us alive together in fellowship and in union with Christ." There's my point again, we all died in Adam, and we shall all be made alive in Christ Jesus.

So, if you haven't accepted Jesus as your savior, you are still under Satan's control: therefore you are incapable of separating your thoughts, and ideas from the influence of the demon spirit.

- THE TRUTH: THE EXTENDED VERSION -

Your only way to life is through Jesus. This is from the Amplified Bible, St. John 1:12 says: "as many as did receive and welcome Him, He gave the authority (power, privilege, right) to become the children of God, that is, to those who believe in (adhere to, trust in, and rely on) His name."

If you haven't accepted Jesus Christ: Please say this Prayer and experience LIFE for the first time. "Jesus I believe you are the Son of God, and I believe you died for my sins, I repent, and turn from my wrong doings. I receive you now as my Lord and savior, and I ask for you to Baptize me with your Holy spirit, I ask this in the precious Name of Jesus Christ, AMEN".